*

Indefatigable

By

J.J. Bhatt

ISBN:

9798870616933

Title:

Indefatigable

Author:

J.J. Bhatt

Published and Distributed by Amazon and
Kindle worldwide.

This book is manufactured in the Unites States of America

Dedicated to
The Brave Breeze,
Bree (1974-2024)
Who indeed shall
Be a shining jewel
Of our love forever.

Recent Books by J.J. Bhatt

HUMAN ENDEAVOR: Essence & Mission/ A Call for Global Awakening, (2011)

ROLLING SPIRITS: *Being Becoming* /A Trilogy, (2012)

ODYSSEY OF THE DAMNED: *A Revolving Destiny,* (2013).

PARISHRAM: Journey of the Human Spirits, (2014).

TRIUMPH OF THE BOLD: *A Poetic Reality*, (2015).

THEATER OF WISDOM, *(2016).*

MAGNIFICENT QUEST: *Life, Death & Eternity,* (2016).

ESSENCE OF INDIA: A Comprehensive Perspective, (2016).

ESSENCE OF CHINA: *Challenges & Possibilities*, (2016).

BEING & MORAL PERSUASION: *A Bolt of Inspiration*, (2017).

REFELCTIONS, RECOLLECTIONS & EXPRESSIONS, (2018).

ONE, TWO, THREE... ETERNITY: *A Poetic Odyssey, (*2018).

INDIA: Journey of Enlightenment, (2019a).

SPINNING MIND, SPINNING TIME: *C'est la vie*, (2019b).Book 1.

MEDITATION ON HOLY TRINITY, *(2019c), Book 2.*

ENLIGHTENMENT: *Fiat lux*, (2019d), Book 3.

BEING IN THE CONTEXTUAL ORBIT: *Rhythm, Melody & Meaning, (*2019e).

QUINTESSENCE: *Thought & Action,* (2019f).

THE WILL TO ASCENT: *Power of Boldness & Genius,* (2019g).

RIDE ON A SPINNING WHEEL: *Existence Introspected, (*2020a).

A FLASH OF LIGHT: Splendors, Perplexities & Riddles, (2020b).

ON A ZIG ZAG TRAIL: *The Flow of Life*, (2020c).

UNBOUNDED: An Inner Sense of Destiny (2020d).

REVERBERATIONS: The *Cosmic Pulse,* (2020e).

LIGHT & DARK: *Dialogue and Meaning,* (2021a).

ROLLING REALITY: Being in flux, (2021b).

FORMAL SPLENDOR: *The Inner Rigor,* (2021c).

TEMPORAL TO ETERNAL: *Unknown Expedition,* (2021d).

TRAILBLAZERS: *Spears of Courage*, (2021e).

TRIALS & ERRORS: A Path to Human Understanding, (2021f).

MEASURE OF HUMAN EXPERIENCE: *Brief Notes,* (2021g).

LIFE: An Ellipsis (2022a).

VALIDATION: The Inner Realm of Essence (2022b).

LET'S ROLL: *Brave Heart,* (2022c). /

DISCOURSE: *Being & Mission* (2022d).

BEING BECOMING, (2022e).

ESSENTIAL HUMANITY: *A Conceptual Clarity* (2022f)

INVINCIBLE, (2022g).

THE CODE: *DESTINY,* (2022h).

LIFE DIMYSTIFIED, (2022i)

ESSENTIAL HUMANITY, (2022h).

EPHEMERAL SPLENDOR, (2023a)

CHAOTIC *HARMONY*, (2023b).

INTELLECTUAL MYSTICISM, (2023C).

WILL TO BELIEVE (2023D).

EXPECTATIONS & REALITY, (2023E).

THREAD THAT BINDS, (2023F).

ONCE & FOREVER, (2023G).

PERPLEXED, (2023H)

GO BEYOND, (2023i)

BEING & JOURNEY (2023j

LIFE: *AN ETERNAL HYMN,* (2023k)

INDEFATIGA~~BLE~~, (2024a).

COSMIC PULSE, {2024b).

SWIRLING WINDS, (2024c).

BLINDING BRILLIANCE (2024d).

PREFACE

INDEFATIGBE raises the relevant issue that we are born to consecrate our respective life to truth, courage and meaning, "Who we are and what we ought to be."

This stated goal got to be the first step to the motivated young individuals to roll forward while holding their moral fortitude and rational goodwill. Let them be the indefatigable charioteers of durable peace, hope and harmony.

J.J. Bhatt

8

CONTENTS

Now or Never

It's
The same path
Where stubborn habits
Keep returning now and
Then

All flaring-up into
Violence's, wars and
Genocides, time after
Time

What a shameful
Theme; popping-up,
Life after life

Isn't
There a conscience;
Realizing,
"We're on a path to
Our collective death?"

Isn't
There a thought
To change the deadly
Course we've been on!

Image in Mirror

Goodwill is the
Way to real freedom,
But ain't happening

Alas, contradictions
Prevail whence suffering
Is the consequence

Wisdom is in every
Human, but it's the
Implementation remains
A big obstacle

Everyone got the
Kindness yet it never
Pours out to help others
In the time of need

It's been all talk and
More talks, but no walk
Along the path of good
Whence suffering remains…

Confession

I write 'cause,
I remain in a prolong
Mode of meditation

I write 'cause
It's the royal road
To know my place in
The holistic realm

I write 'cause
It's the light guiding,
"I" through the dark

I write 'cause
While I journey
Between life and
Eternity

I write 'cause
I feel fully free to
Express my thoughts
And be in the effloresce
Bliss forever…

Chameleon

Oh yes.
This crazy notion
Called, "Truth"

What an
Obsession of the
Human soul

That
Elusive "Truth"
Sometimes so-near,

Sometimes
Dancing beyond
My conception

"Truth"
What a
Mystical magic,

Yet
A paradox to my
Ever Searching Soul…

Betrayal

Let us
Visit dear God,
Who is an eternal love or
Just another invention
Of the fearful mind or
What?

Either He is
With us or He isn't
Still a long time issue
Between theists and
Atheists, alright

Poor God,
Abused by his servants;
Peddling their pseudo claims
And falsified narratives to
Control many millions

Take a glimpse
At the world history, and
You will vividly see

Their silent crimes
In the mirror of world history
Fingerprinted by violence's
And the bloody wars, time after
Time..."

Nova Prayer

Let us
Begin another day with
A new prayer:

We're born
To live with a right purpose;
Building
Humanity of unity and
Peace

Let us
Strengthen our collective
Will to enjoy life full of
Hope and happiness from
This point on

Let us
Leave "Good" as a gift to
The young who in turn
Shall continue to inspire their
Descendants for sure

Time to
Wake-up, and change the
World for the greater good
Through our collective effort...

Identity

We're
Timeless travelers
Walking through all
The virtues and vices;
We gain and lose 'em,
Now and then

And, still
We dare to unveil the
Mystery of our collective
Essence, so well

Like it or not,
We're the moral braves
Walking through the
Eternal chaotic harmony
And we never quit the
Scene

Oh yes,
We're the lost tribe of
Contradictions, riddles…
Subjective interpretations,

Yet we
Prevail with our
Indomitable will to
Win, no matter what?

Urbane

Life
What a continuum
Poetry in motion
Forever

That's the
Way, I look at it
From my vantage
Point of view

Poetry
What a sweet and
Bitter feelings of
Human existence

Poetry
What an Inspiring
Song to the young and
Old, rich and poor or
Whoever,

I mean, if they
Care to be free from the
"Techno-addictions,"
Of course!

Let's Change

Why don't
We be the spiraling
Odyssey of truth

Why don't
We come together
And dismiss the old
War mongering habit
Of all

Let us
Wipe off the sinful
Past and get ready to
Paint a new profile,
"Peace and hope"

Let us
Build a new spirit "One
Humanity, One Planet
To keep clean, and One
Moral force of Good"

We've Sinned

Let's
Reverberate the
Sleepy world with
Ever renewable spirit:

Our set
Mission and endeavor
Are inseparable indeed
For that's the only way
To conquer the quest

That's how
Our collective will can
Lead us to the
Highway of Perfection

Let's open the
Rational mind and
Reckon,

"It's the ignorance
And falling for the
Pseudo worship; blinding
The mind for too long."

Great Paradox

Love,
What a beautiful
Gift to cherish

Love,
The way to real
Human to be

Love,
The blend of
Ecstasy and agony,
Never to forget

Love,
"What a double-
Edged experience"

Love,
What a passion,
In it lovers die
By the millions...

Believe

We're
Indefatigable
Heroes of our time

No matter
How long to embattle
Evil to make room
For "Good"

Time to
Drop the defeatist
Attitude and fear of
Death

Time to
Pull together our
Collective strength

And conquer the
Ever turbulent mind,
And be the victors at
This turning point...

Being & Essence

Real virtue is
Not knowledge, but
The poetic expression;

Let every
Mind enjoy creative
Freedom so fearlessly
Indeed

Serendipity is
Another mighty;
Opening door to the
Many possibilities

A bold moral
Stand against injustice
Also is a shining freedom
Shown by a few great souls

Poetry is
A force of freedom. It's
Not cheap. It's not rights
And privileges...it's the
Fortitude to take on any
Evil face to face...

Ultimate
Light

In time,
All things must be
Reduced to their
Essences

All struggles,
And despairs
Must end

Let there be
A new dawn
Let there be
Ultimate Light;

Waking-up
Ignorant humans
From their
Repeated blunders
And sins, and be the
Moral Spirits again…

The
Climb

Let
Victory opens up
Its mighty arms, so I
Can touch my truth

As I encounter
High mountains on
The way

I must know,
The climb is subtle
And complex indeed

But I don't care
For 'am ready to
Journey to know
My truth

It's all about
Measuring the will
Through logical
Connectivity with the
Whole…

Double-edged

Life
Brings beautiful
Lyrics and deep
Memories as the
Precious gifts

It also
Gives agony and
Despair
Not easy to heal

That's the
Double-edged sword,
Call it, the journey of
"Human spirit"

Life is
Meaningful only
When humanity
Sustains integrity,
Civility and dignity
Of all for a long…

Deathless

Man is
Constantly
Writing his destiny
As he rolls from
Life toward death

He
Demands direction
To walk through rough
Terrain

Human
What a wonderful
Inner reality; dictating
His dream

Human,
Always in search of
His authentic identity,
And the journey never
Ends...

Being:
An Idea

An idea
Must have an ethical
Value

Only then,
Human is worthy of his
Journey toward higher
Goals

An idea is
Noble if it is "All
Inclusive" benefitting
Billon others too

Human is
An idea that has
Accidently landed on
This Plane Blue

Human
Alone must define,
"Who he is and what
He ought to be?"

Off the Edge

Let
Meditation
Be the path

Let it be
In harmony with
All that is

Let's
Take a stand in the
Name of a meaningful
Existence

Let it be
The evolving moral
Intention to make
Some difference

Come,
Let's walk together
To be one precious
Humanity forever.

Toward Future

Let
Young be inspired
Every way and
Let 'em soars
Through beauty and
Truth at this time

Encourage
'Em to rise high above
Cacophony, chaos
And greed

Let 'em
Purify their souls
Let 'em
Prepare for their
Ultimate victory to
The end

Let 'em
Fly high above
Bickering, frictions and
False narratives at this time...

Be Bold

Why
Is this place
Of tears and
Struggles?

Why not
The place of reason
And common sense!

Don't let the
Naysayers impose
Their will

Don't let the
Irrational believers
Throw
You off the trail

Stay focused
While passing through
The dark patch

Keep
Rolling, keep
Evolving…keep the
Chin-up till the mission
Is conquered at last…

New Chapter

Time
To validate our
Collective will to move
The mighty mounts

Time to fight
Excessive: greed, vanity
And ignorance and more

Time to
Reset new ways, new
Vigor and new future
For the kids

Time to
Dismiss all the
Violent narratives and

Time to
Clear the way for the
Young to live
In the world of rhythms,
Melodies and meaning
For a change...

Explorers

Voila,
This is the mystical
Reality

Where
Humans are offer
One time rare gift

To roll
Along the axis of life
And death with a firm
Purpose

Discover it
While the journey's on
And you'll be the hero
Of your own walk

That is the
Magic of all time
That is the
Answer to the
Abstruse existence
Alright…

To Be

Each born
Is an enlightened
Soul to be

Each
Struggling
Got the power
To change the
World indeed

Each is a
Moral poetry in
Motion;
Bringing truth,
"All that is"

Each is a
Friend and a foe
At the same time
In existence

Let each be
Aware, "How to
Conquer the monkey
Mind always!"

Wake-up

Don't
Fall for their
Irrelevance, but
Learn to think,
"Instead"

Just discover,
What is it all about?
With your own logical
Insight and pure
Courage

Remember,
There ain't a blissful
Paradise up there
There ain't
Beauties waiting
Either

Wake-up
From the imposed
Fantasy, and be with a
Reason driven faith...

Mind
Opener

My child asked,
"Dad, what is hell?"

Well, I thought for
A while and replied:

Hell is where
There is no love, but
Evil is the norm

Hell is
Where humanity
Loses its dignity,
Civility and integrity
At the same time

"Dad, that means
We've to pay the price
For our sins?"

"Of course, that is the
Unwritten law of life…"

The child shot back,
"If I can understand,
Why don't the grown-ups?"

Off the Nightmare

Time
To ride the rising
Tide of change while
Facing it now and then

Let there
Be a new gusto, yes a
New spirit to reach out
The envisioned goal

No point
In repeating the old
Habit of violence's and
Wars

Time to
Leave the dark state
And begin to look
Beyond…

Time to
Act

Come,
Ladies and
Gentlemen

Let's
Ensure our
Confidence
And a firm stand
Today

Many
Struggles shall
Ebb and flow in
Many tomorrows

Come on,
Ladies and
Gentlemen, time is
Here to save our losing
Essence in this world
Of ever in turbulence…

The Flesh

She's an
Irresistible beauty
With great pizzazz

Where ever
She lands, she draws
Attention of million
Men

She's smart,
Well-educated and
Very sophisticated
Teaser to the
Many waiting hearts

She's
The young wife of
The big corporate boss
And she enjoys
Splurging his billions
And she doesn't care

If the
Hubby is dead or
Alive so long she got
There craving material
Wants...

Truth as is

Divinity,
What a mysterious
Human spirit per se

It's the
Reason to be
It's the
Justification
To be

Indeed,
That's the way
To be yet

Sadly, humans
Not grasping it
At all,

"Divinity is the
Holistic connectivity
Where unity is the
Ultimate."

Whence
Much darkness in
Our time…

Introspection

Only in
Purity of love,
There is a possibility
To know my truth

Only in
Sincerity of purpose;
Opening my passage
To the paradise only

Yes,
The trail is long and
Must keep walking with
A determined will

Time
To paint a nova image,
A new vision, new thoughts
To gain a rational insight

Remember,
"We are known and the
Unknown" through the
Lenses of our
Imperfect beliefs...

Inseparable

Dear Heart,
I stand to give my
Life in the name of
Our eternal love

Yes, dear Heart
We're born to be
One from the very
Start

When we
Danced and kissed
For the first time;
We knew,
"What it meant"

Life after
Life, love has been
The meaning of you
And I

I say, "Please
Don't leave me alone
Here while you wait
In eternity…"

Love, what a
Wonderful magic
Between two souls,
Called, "You and me."

Being & Reality

Reality is
Nothing, but where
Everything unfolds

From
Great riddles
To the anticipated
Perfection

In such a
Labyrinthine web of
Complexity; time is
A first deception

Also in such an
Abstruse state of
Everything

Intelligent being
Keeps rolling forward,
With his big query,
"What is it all about?"

Wrong
Way

What a
Tragedy to the good
Souls of the Earth

Where billions
Seek peace, harmony
And security to live,
But not able to experience

While a few
Loaded with power,
Wealth and greed are
Navigating the big ship

In our time,
It's not so different
From the past as
Same old stratagem
Continues with greater
Intensity, of course

Oh this
Thick pile of violence's,
Wars and even genocides;
Killing the genuine humanity
Every time…

Red Flag

Whenever
Super smart
Thinking machines keep
Gaining their hold over
Humanity

That is the
Time every concerned
Citizen must take a bold
Stand and fight for their
Freedom

If not,
The evil forces would
Silently swallow up
Our dignity, our integrity,
Our civility and in fact,
Our very humanity

Time to
Act now or never
Time to walk the walk
Today, but not to wait
Until tomorrow…

Cosmic Glimpse

Nothing is
Either pure or
Simple in the
Universe

We're here
Accidentally, and
Keep colliding with
Uncertainty and
Destructiveness,
Evidently

In such a
World, death
Got no meaning for
It's just recurrences
From one
Beginning to another,
Ad infinitum

After all,
In the womb,
"Humanity begins
With a tiny cosmic
Spark!"

Being & Existence

Existence
Means,
I am a
Journey

Existence
Means,
I am the
Reality

Existence
Means,
I am the
Essence;

Leading
"I" to
The holistic
"All that is"

Reflection

As we walk
Forward through
Our given time

All seems
Non sequitur,
Inchoate and

Disturbing
To our
Silent Souls

Why we're
The wounded
Spirits;

And why
We're struggling
Through the
Serrated terrain?

Why don't
We grasp,
"We're the
Ultimate unity
Of all differences."

Mystical

"I"
A formidable will
Who is stubborn to
Quit the scene

"I"
What a spiritual
Spark; illuminating
All that is dark

"I"
Never reconciles
With forces of the
Stygian night

"I"
What an eternal
Magic Soul destined
To show the path,
Life after life…

Petite Fleur

Hey gal,
Don't you recall?
"We're in love many
Times before?"

Hey sweet
Gal, don't you know
"We've been in love
Life after life"

I say,
"Don't ignore our
Friendship of many
Gone by days"

Come,
Dear love and
Open up your heart
Once again

Dear petite
Fleur,
"Love is immortal,
So are we indeed…"

Great Wheel

What if
This birth, death and
Rebirth must be a
Cosmic thread tying
"I" in the ever
Holistic experience!

As the
Great Wheel
Keeps spinning, "I"
Turns into an ever
Exploring
Consciousness

It's all about
Knowing, "Why
My Mystic Self
Continues to be
Reincarnated
Birth after Birth?"

Forever

Yes,
I do think of that
Sweet girl
She's a live universe
Of ever beauty indeed

Oh yes,
I'd asked her,
"Come and
Dance with me for our
Destiny was waiting"

Yes,
We began another bold
Journey from that
Memorable moment on

I reminded
Her, "Please don't
Ignore this guy who
Loves you more than
You'll ever know"

Well,
She heeded
To my feelings, and we
Have been dancing forever,
Forever…forever since…

Rare Avis

Being is
Always a querying
Mind

Driven by
Endless curiosity
And determined will

He's
Poetry in motion
Who dares to touch
Core of the unknown

And, his
Journey; what a magic

Rhythms, melodies and
Meaning

Let him
Continue to go beyond
Cacophony and despair

Let him
Experience first-hand,
"He's the ultimate Spirit
In the Universe…"

Persevere

It has been
A long walk to the
Temple of Enlightenment

It took
Million births to seek
The truth, "What is it all
About?"

And, still
To face the same old
Dilemmas and the
Subjective interpretations;
To grasp it all,

"Who we are and
Where are we heading from
Here to wherever is beyond?"

By the way,
It has been a long journey
To reckon,

"There is a dire
Need to strengthen our moral
Will to win the tough times…"

Change
The Track

Let it be
Vividly understood,
"Compassion is a
Strong and not an idealized
Notion

Albeit it's a logical
Necessity for the survival
Of humanity itself"

In a long run,
Only compassion brings
Hope, courage and dignity
To every man, woman and
Child

And not
Lies, pseudo-worships
And dogmatic claims for
They give nothing, but
Bigotry, violence's and
Wars in return

Sadly, misguided
Zealots keeps killing
Many innocent,
Poor and very young...

Being As Is

Oh yes,
Every ontological
Being seeking,
"What is a genuine
Soul?"

To understand
It, he, must be
The set quest

Being means
All thoughts,
Curiosities and
Consequences

Every born
Is purity at the
Core and must
Be inspired for
Good

Every being
Waiting to be
Validated before
Passing on to another
Realm...

Zombies

So long
There is uncertainty
Of human identity,
There shall
Be chaotic harmony
In the world

All intentions,
Goals and events shall
Be subjected to decay
And decadence

There shall be
A grand amnesia as
Humans continues with
Their unworkable rules
Of the game

No wonder,
Why Humanity is
Losing its moral vigor,
Harmony and hope

Why have we
Forgotten our individual
Divinity, and why turned
Into zombies; neglecting the
Future of innocent kids!

Upwelling

Oh yes,
This permanent
Obsession named,
"Truth"

Always
Full o intrigue
And so challenging
To unfold

Truth,
What a mental magnet
Where all thoughts
Roll

Indeed,
Truth must be our
Moral alter-ego;

Guiding
Toward the eternal
"Self-realization"

Truth
Not a divinity, but
Human endeavor…it's
Just an idea emerging
From the soul…

History
Singing

Existence is
Trapped between
"Good and Evil"

Good is
What yields hope,
Harmony and Peace;

Opening the
Way to myriad
Great possibilities,
Beauty and dreams

Evil is
Choices bringing
Fragmentations,
Destructions and deaths

History still singing,
"Why we're suffering
Even, today?"

Children demanding,
"Please be on the
Side of good for our
Sake..."

Accidental

It all
Exploded instantly
From no-where

And the
Cosmic pulse began
Throbbing ever since

Whatever
Appeared, soon took
Its shape and form

Well, there
Manifested the most
Colorful and chaotic
Universe

Human,
Just one of the infinite
Flares from mother Fire

Whose
Still looking to grasp
The meaning of his
Essence, but no answer
Yet to report...

Echoes

What the
Wise already
Said many times
Before "I" is
Just another
Cosmic echo

"I" tried to
Grasp essences
Of all that is

"I" sought
All possibilities
Together ahead

Well, "I" is
At the edge, and
Ready to fly off
To the source...

Be Smart

If a man is
Not insulted a few
Times
He won't
Appreciate,
"What is the value of
Respecting others"

If a man
Doesn't go through
The agony of defeat,
"He won't know the
Value of his victory"

If a man
Doesn't fall in love
And be burned by it,
"He won't feel depth of
His humanity"

If a man,
Doesn't grasp the
Truth of his woman,
"He won't know what
Is the meaning of his
Essence in life…"

Synopsis

Only
In his conceptual
State of the mind,
"There is divinity,
Truth and beauty"

Once,
He' freed
From the mental
Sphere, everything
Must disappear in
An instant"

Only in
The metaphysical
Experience,
"Magnifique Unity
Remains an ever
Supreme Reality

In fact, without
Any brand names,
Dogmas and diabolic
Intentions…"

Self-Image

No need to
Measure the Divine
For your follies, but
The onerous is upon
You only

No need to
Criticize Him,
Now and then for your
Quasi-animal conduct;
That you're essentially

Don't
Blame the Divine
For your divisional
Frictional mentality,
But to your kind simply

Don't
Keep complaining
Against the Divine
For your blunders and
Many recurring sins;
Frankly speaking...

Illumination

Let there be
Light in every heart,
Mind and soul

Let there be
Enlightened beings
To be a norm, and

Don't let
Negative forces
To erase your
Moral will ever

Stay calm and
Be alert for the
World is

Burdened
By the zillion tons
Of vanity, vengeance
And greed...

New Journey

**Still
Keep the bold stand,
And be powered
By the Deathless
Will**

**Let's
Forgive the inherited
Sins, but never
Forget them**

**Let's
Focus the present,
And roll toward
The noble mission**

**Let's
Relearn to drop the
"Dark necessity," and
Be the moral essence**

**Let it be the
Moral calling and
Let it be the awakened
A new journey from this
Moment on...**

Some
Ideas

Constant
Conflicting ideas
Sets
The creative forces
In motion

I mean,
Ideas of God,
Universe, morality
And the being
Himself

Ideas,
Oh yes that great
Obsession of thinking
Beings;

Defining the very
Rationale to be the
Innovative Humans,
Indeed

Let illumined
Ideas lift humans to
Their beauty and truth...

Love
101 Not

It was in the
Romantic storm,
We'd lost our track

And, there was
Nowhere to go, but
To the bleeding heart

It was
A deception,
It was a fake apology
That never healed

I was just a
Misunderstanding
May be a
Mistrust that kept
Repeating and we
Kept dying every time…

Pure
Love

Your aura,
What a regal beauty;
Sparkling as ever since
We've been in love

What a
Scintillating is
Her mind, always
Extending understanding
At every step

Oh yes,
I am the luckiest guy
Being in love with such
A lovely heart

No more
/She's a dream, but
Reality that has fallen
In my laps

Damn right,
I am the luckiest guy,
Who's not dreaming, but
Experiencing purity of love
From here to infinity…

Endeavor

Fate,
Mustn't be a
Way out from personal
Responsibility

Fate,
Mustn't be refuge to
Seek sympathy

Nothing be
Justified for escapism,
But human endeavor only

Let's
Come alive with
Power of moral call
For a better world

Let
Human be guided
By the basic code of
Conduct, and

Let his
Cooperative spirit
Do the magic till the
End...

Exit

Each being,
An intricately woven
Living fabric of good
And evil

Those awakened
Know the value of
Good benefiting the
Whole

That would
Be the turning point
To be illumined

Otherwise,
The present scenario
If continues;
Evil forces shall shore up
Destructions and deaths...

Let it Glow

It's
Existence that shall
Evolve our thoughts,
Words and deeds to
The world of many
Unknowns

What is a
Human life but a
Momentary ambition
To be validated by the
Societal others

Indeed,
It's a passing phase of
Obsession of triumphs,
Controls and tribal claims

Existence
Not meant to be
Wasted in the glory
Of a geographic god

Its mission is
To build a safe world of
Harmony and peace via
"Self-awakening" while
The rides on...

Lesson to Remember

At the
Height of most
Civilizations, humanity
Remained relevant for
Their ideals and moral
Commitments

Well, that is the
Impression, history
Gives us to be inspired
And to learn a lesson or
Two, I guess

There were
Once the Egyptians,
The Sumerians, the
Persians, the Athenians,
The Romans and so on

Well,
We know, how each
Got busted by the silent
Decay and decadence

Let each
Ambitious nation take note,
"Beware of the past and
Shape- up as soon it must…"

Alternate Track

What we
Must learn is not the
Glorious adventures
Of winning the bloody wars,
But its understanding, not
Repeating the follies from the
Past

History is
Essentially a warning
Sign that we must read it
Every time and rethink
When triggering another
Bloody war either
Big or small

In every war,
Many innocent dies and
Those living carries the
Burden for a long

Only
Peace brings healing,
Understanding and unity
Within diversity of incessant
Conflicts...

Be
Inspired

Young Braves,
Go where you're
The meaning of
Your noble birth

Let your
Bold spirit walk
Along the moral trail,
And be a mighty one

Don't let
The cacophony of
Destructive narratives
Disturb your focus point

I say,
"Hold your head
High as you roll toward
Your well defined goal...

The Way

If we
Just take it with a
Positive flare

That would
Be the first step to
Evolve toward a world
Of rational insight

That is the way,
To go from confusion to
Clarity, and from
Ignorance to awakening

After all,
We must make every
Effort to live with joy,
And

Not grief
As life takes us
From the darkness to
The brilliant starlight...

Sunshine

There is
Sunshine,
There is you and
I and our Truth

There is
Spring smiling
With many dreams;
Inviting us to be part
Of it forever

There is
You and I whose
In love from the
Very first smile

Oh yes,
My lovely soul
You're perfection,
Wishes and dreams

"Cone let's
Dance with the fullest
Happiness forever…"

Essential Being

Time
To be renewed
Time to be
Self-confident

We're
The historic-force
In- making and

We must,
Be direction
OF our common
Destiny

Don't run
Away from moral
Challenges

Don't ever run
Away from social
Responsibility

For you're
To build a better
World for children to
Be happy for a very long...

Ebb & Flow

Nothing so
New only we come,
Stay for a while and
We go

That is
The brief length of
Our journey from
Cradle to the death

Though it's
A short trip, but got
Million challenges
To fulfill

Be smart,
Be aware of your
Time, and act as if
It's the last day to
Be alive

Life, what a
Teaser….life what
A hidden gem that's
Reveled so late…

Relevance

We exists
To bring clarity
To our complex web of
Misunderstandings

Indeed,
We're suffering
"Cause we've forgotten
Our genuine identity"

We've been
Running wild along
A wrong track

As the
Bloody history keeps
Reminding at all
The time

We're
Miserable's whose
Still walking through
The dark tunnel, and not
Knowing that we're!

Divided
We Die

Each
Thought silently
Builds an idea and
In turn an opinion

Bunch of
Opinions' define the
Way we understand
Our world

It's called,
"The world view" and
Each keeps blowing
His point of view

Oh yes,
Each powered by
Myopic expression, and
Each holding a stubborn
Stand for a selfish aim

So, we fail to
Lift humanity to
Its ultimate unity,
"What is our truth."

Get Smart

No
Need to judge,
Take the responsibility
Instead and move on

No need
To claim victory
Instead take care of
Poor, hungry and sick

No need
To trigger wars when
Millions die for nothing
And never healing the
Wounds

No need
To declare independence,
If humans are subjugated
By the ultra-modern-thinking
Machines'

No need
To use God, a panacea
For all our inglorious
Cruelties, time after
Time…

The Territory

Truth is
Visible when we
Act morally right and
Rationally with a
Sincerity of purpose

God is
Alive and good when
We fight for harmony
And peace

Love is
Immortal when we
Never fail in trust and
Friendship

Life is a
Meaning, when we
Understand the value
Of our global mission in
Time...

Pursuit

We're
Evolving souls
As we flow from here
To somewhere that we
Really don't know

We're the
Lost one who hasn't
Grasped the genuine
Identity at this point

Though
We're indefatigable,
Yet we wear out
Thin when it comes
To meet the moral call

Let's regain
Our humanity,
Yes our mystical beauty

I say,
"Let's discover our
Selves before we go off
The scene…"

Be
Confident

Only in
Love we shall
Either live or die

So dear Heart,
"Why let go our beautiful
Affairs in
Such hurry at this point?"

Only in
Our proven friendship,
" Now we're the One
Out of two souls"

I know,
Journey's been
Arduous, but this is the
Time to believe in the
Depth of our love

Come
Dear Heart, let's
Clarify the state of our
Troubled affair, and let's
Roll toward our common
Destiny again...

Change,
The Way

**Time to
Recapture the
"Self-knowledge;"
Paving way for
"Awakening"**

**Of course,
Awakening in turn;
Bringing truth alive
Through
The moral action**

**In mean,
"Without
Self-knowledge,"
We're not real.
We're not relevant...**

Where?

Where
Do we begin our
Quest

I mean,
"When do we
Fly off the edge?"

In this
Magnifique Universe
Where do we seek
Our meaning?

Who should
We rely either the
Belief or the silent
Soul!

Where
Do we begin the
Journey we're on

Why pursue
To know the meaning
When uncertainty is
Sovereign as our truth? Where

The Gist

In the big
Picture, "What is?"
Where moral intention
Matters

In the big
Riddle of all that is,
Only rational goodwill
Is the real force

It was
A blunder to keep
Apart; Divine and
Humans through
Deceptive narratives

It was
Not wise to ignore the
Destructive habits of the
Few greedy minds

Still time is
To save our kind and
Be free from the clutches
Of despair we're in…

Eternal

In this
Inscrutable existence,
"I" is my consciousness;
Leading me to the temple
Of waiting truth

Yes, "I" is my
Mystical spirit, albeit
My freewill and moral
Integrity alright

It's been
A long journey and
Still many more to go

That's the
The direction,
"I" must roll and

Let "I" reveal
Its eternal essence
Before my time to go...

Barrier

Salute to
Those desiring
Peace, freedom and
Justice to all

Salute to
All the great ideas
Bringing harmony and
Hope to all

Glad every human
Got the same inner
Wish to see the world
To b good

Only issue,
Ideal wishes and
Dreams often fail
'Cause humans expect
Others to do
The job for them

They talk and
Offer more talks, but
Not ready to walk the
Walk... what a pity!

Be Bold

Exuberant,
Of course we are
As ever

Self-directed
Light; damn right
We can

We're the
Totality of whatever
It was, it is and shall
Be

In essence,
We're timeless born
And reborn from
Place to place

Existence,
Simply an expression
Of our inner voice

Let us
Be bold to know, "Who
We're and what we can
Become..."

Give a Damn

How
Thrilling it is
To reckon, "We're
The New Dawn"

Neither
Individualism nor
A family to think
For we've to be the
"Global Spirit"

Look at
The Planet Blue in
Need of desperate help
Look at
The history full of
Bad choices and deeds

Today,
Humanity and the
Earth are facing serious
Existential threat

Let's roll-up the
Sleeves…let's join hands
And be illuminated at this
Turning point of our
Precious time…

Hello
Lady M

Only
In your love,
There is a meaning to
Journey through this
Illogical existence

Only
In your selflessness
And infinite inner
Strength

I find
A full inspiration
To move on with a
Full-confidence

Oh yes,
Dear love,
It is through your
Goodness and
Endless care

My existence...my
Very essence been
Justified to the core...

Authentic

The value of
A real faith is in its
Open-mindfulness, and
In the firm commitment
To non-violence

That is
The responsibility of
Every human to hold
As their ground

That is
The gateway to the
"Enlightened World"
And that is the moral
Call

Ignore those
Peddling
False narratives and
Failed experiment

Killing\
In the name of
A merciful Divine is a
Contradiction and a big sin
Itself…

Being &
Destiny

To grasp
The totality of my
Reality
I am reborn
As a simple gift;
To think outside
The box

Yes,
To seek essence
Within million riddles
Of existence, and
That is
Where moral will
Turns wisdom, and

In turn,
Gets me off the
Stubborn chaos and the
Senseless ego trips

Clarity of
Thoughts, words and
Vision take time, but
They propelled me toward,
"What is my meaning in
This grand scheme of
Things?"

Surprise

What if,
Human is the only
Living spark in the
Universe

Who got
The capacity to think,
To understand and to
Envision the future

But then, it's a
Paradox for he has
Not arrived there yet!

What if,
Human is the only
Inheritor to unlock all
The mysteries of the
Teasing reality?

Given the chaos
Of our time, sadly
He has not even begun
To reckon his infinite
Possibilities yet!

Human Mission

At the
Center of the issue,
"To conquer the mind
Must be the supreme
Mission"

That's the way
To set the noble goal,
And move on along the
Right track

Oh yes,
Let's be the Impossible
Possible, and be the master
Of our collective destiny at
This point

No reason
Fighting for the Unknown
Divine and no reason to
Keep living with a
Divided mindset

Let's deliver
Good to the world, and
Fulfill the mission we've
Been destined to do it
Just that...

Just
A Tweak

Simply
Change the godly
Equation to something
Called, "Moral Good"

And, with such a
Common sense, let's
Spin the wheel of civility
Integrity and delayed
Awakening at once

Please,
Change the simple
State of the mind, and
Believe in the logical
Necessity to be calm and
Courteous for a change

Come let's bring
Heavenly Peace on
Earth....yes to make the
Mortal being "Good," again,
And not someone else!

Action
Time

Time
To walk along a
Trail leading to
Peace and order
At once

Outside of it,
All is t talk and more
Talks and nothing
Good in return to gain

Why aren't
We concerned with
Disenchantment
Most everywhere

Why do we
Avoid destruction
Of our humanity by the
Super machines

Time
To take collective
Action and let's
Begin to fulfill our
Dream…

Guiding Force

No point
Thriving in illusion and
Not knowing the right
Path

Life is meant
To be refined as our
Collective responsibility,
Alright

I mean,
Knowing, "What is
The intention of
Our being here?"

No point
Thriving in the dark;
Ignoring the intelligent
Supreme in us

After all life is
All about reckoning,
"Harmony, Happiness and
Full-confidence to live well…"

Oh the Paradise!

Folks still
Believe there is a
Celestial paradise called,
"Heavenly Happiness"

That abode of purity
And full of eternal bliss
Where nothing goes wrong

Every one
Dreams to go there
And be the Perfect beings
Forever

Well, that's the
Fantasy created by
The cleaver religio-doses
To control the herd

Time to
Face truth and time
To awake others, and

Yes, it's time to
Build a paradise with our
Virtues and endeavors....

Derailed

Why exist
In the world of enigmas,
And contradictions powered
By off and on illusions

Why keep
Spinning in the sphere of
Deceptions, lies and greed

Why not
Free the mind from
Destructive thoughts and

Why not
Ascend to the
World of common sense

Why not
Join hands and move
The mountains with our
Collective mighty strength...

Genuine

Many
Published heroes
Are overly
Inflated egos

Well, real heroes
Emerges one or two
Per century

Yes,
The genuine
Heroes simply
Live and die for the
Wellbeing of billion
Others

What a sad story,
Only handful heroes
Came and gone from
Us many billions!

Our Time

The United Nations
Came into being soon
After the World War

At that moment,
There was a unanimous
Agreement: "War is the
Creation of human mind,
And must be eradicated
Permanently…"

Over the years
This great institution got
Corrupted by the "Veto"
Of the few;

Transforming
"United Something to the
United Nothing"

As the
World's been plagued
By violence's, wars and
Even genocides, time after
Time…

Magnifique
Spirit

In her
Warmest smile,
Only happiness keeps
Dancing forever

Yes, that is
"What love ought
To be"

Indeed,
In her sacrifices,
I felt her genuine
Love always

Oh yes,
"I am the luckiest
Guy having won her
"Magnificent Heart"

Rule 101

Why should
I die for I've million
Miles yet to go

Why should
I let go my ideas for
Millions yet to share

Indeed,
The journey's been
Full of struggles, but
Quite exciting as well

That is
The rule 101 of life;
Won't be changing
For a while

Life
Must be the
Trail of meditation;
Rediscovering the Self
Over and again till
The mind is illumined...

Worthy Being

Being's
Core essence is his
Authentic identity and
That's where
His journey begins

That's how he's
Inspired to succeed
In seeking his "Truth"

Human essence is
The metaphysical
Fingerprint meant to
His ultimate triumph

Let
His essence be the
Real freedom from the
World of illusion,
Narcissism and hypocricy...

Being & Purpose

Totality of
Reality is grasped
Through
"Self-consciousness"

I mean,
Through a perceptual
And a meditative being,
Of course

"I" never
A regretful error, but
A glowing spark
Of every soul

Human journey is
To heal, to love and
To conquer the troubled
Mind birth after birth;
Essentially...

Don't
Hijack

Value of
Faith is in its
Kindness and
Forgiveness

That is the
Only way to lift
Humans from their
Recurring sins

Value of faith
Is in its believers to
Be illuminated;

Dismissing
The false narratives:
Vanity, vengeance
And greed

Faith is valid when
Peace, harmony and
Hope equals humanity
In its full moral sense...

Validation

So that is
All about our
Justification to be
Humans

I mean,
To know something
Of the unknown called,
"God" and

To explore
All possibilities to reach
The Temple, "VERITAS"

Yes,
To lift the humanity
And validate it,
"Above all"

To leave a
Legacy; inspiring
The young

To carry on
The torch of hope,
Self-confidence and
Integrity of the mind
Forever...

Soaring
High

I am just
Another rolling
Spirit of my wishes
And dreams

Indeed,
I am just an
Another struggling
Stranger

Journeying
With billion others
Through my time

Certainly am
Lost into the constant
Chaos and endless
Subjectivity of all kinds…

First Step

How do we
Go steady in the world
When uncertainty remains
Sovereign

Why do we
Care to meet the Divine
Who has messed up
Humanity from the start

And how do we
Pursue our ultimate quest
When chaotic milieu is
The reality as always

Where do we
Take the first step and
Be triumphant;

Transcending
From dream to a new
Reality of spiritual tempo,
Melody and meaning...

Serendipity

Maker of
Reality must be the
Human mind itself,
"All that is"

What a
Spontaneous
Awareness of him

What a
Marvelous "Thinking
Being" on the cosmic
Scene

In him,
There is striving to
Seize the meaning

In him,
There is determination
To lit-up the darkness

In him,
There is laughter, love
And many possibilities
To celebrate indeed!

Life & Time

Human mind
Always a
Measuring stick

Of God,
Humanity, religious
Imperfection, and

of course
Many geopolitical
Blunders

At every step,
There is a judgment call
To discern either right or
Wrong, and

At every turning
Point there is a decision
To make either good
Or otherwise

Life and
Time under the moral
Measure either to rise
Or die otherwise…

The Game

A stream of
Thoughts
Silently builds
An idea and

In turn,
Into something
Called, "Opinion"

When bunch
Of opinions tied
Together,
They expressed,
"The World View"

In turn,
Each world view
Rooted in the making
Of a narrative

Each narrative
Fighting for cultural
Superiority

Each narrative
Intends to dominate
Either directly or
Indirectly; controlling
Billion human minds...

The Crux

We're
Freedom when
Making choices

That is the
Only slit open to
Shape our destiny

We
Don't control the
Consequences, but
Face 'em one way
Or other

That's
The crux of human
Existence where
Uncertainty control
The decisions…

Power
To Be

Every
Human is his/her
"Point of view"

But, only few
Who stood through
Action for the good
Of others,

Left their
Marks and we call em
"Heroes of all time"

Every human
So born is the
Symbol of courage
To do some good, and

Every human
Though mortal got
The power to change
The world and be the
Hero of all time...

Poor God

What if,
We changed the
God equation and

What if
We equate Him with
An enlightened humanity

For a long,
God's been misunderstood
For a long,
His name's been abused
By the blood thirsty zealots

Even His
Messages been twisted
To let a few control their
Herds

Poor God's been
Imprisoned by the
Evil doers for a long

And, He's been
Screaming, "Stop
Violence's and wars in
My name"

Pilgrims

Compassion
Must be the only
Answer to
Cure our miserable
Existence

There has to be
Moral courage to tie
The fragmented
Humanity in time

Yes,
There has to be
Willingness to take a
Stand against injustice

There has to be
A concerted effort to
Save dignity of every
Human

Only then
We shall have a
Real meaning to our
Collective pilgrimage…

Reboot

Why exists
In the world of
Contradictions, enigmas
And sheer illusion

Why
Rot in the world of
Ignorance, arrogance
And indifferent attitude

Time
To wake-up, arise and
Get rolling to erase all the
Diseases of yesterday

Time
To inspire the young,
And avoid all the follies of
Their elders

Time,
To live in simplicity, and
Less techno-addicted state

Yes, let humanity
Has a fresh freedom
To breathe...

Yesterday

Can't forget
Days of being
Young and dancing
In the rain

Yes, yes
Those carefree days
Of being in love forever

All was
Possibilities
And no fear to hold
But be in love only

Oh yes,
Those days of
Yesterdays

When
We're young;
Dancing with a fever
Of love, love, love
And love forever.

Blueprint

History
What a wonderful
Rear view to see
Our naked truth,

"How we arrived
From the past to the
Present and what be the
Prospects for the future"

Collectively
We're writing the
History irrespective; what
May be the consequences

History,
What a
Precious blueprint
Handed over from one
Generation to another
Reminding,

"How to
Avoid blunders of
Yesterday by growing up;
Very soon..."

Will to Believe

I am
Here to believe,
Life's been a great
Voyage even through
The rough Sea

Like any other,
I faced a few trials and
Trepidations, but I've
Assailed in the end

It's been a
Great learning, it's been
A challenging journey and
It's been a deep reckoning

For which I express my
Gratitude for having born
Human time after time…

Unknown

Death is
Sacred
Death is
Freedom and
It's a universal
Equalizer to the end

Death is
A final receptor
Where the past and the
Present are voided in
An instant

Death
What a wonderful
Passage to the
The great spinning
Wheel forever...

First Spark

Let the world
Take note:
Poetry is an eternal
Light being intricately
Woven with the soul
And truth

Poetry is
A moral necessity
Of every born for
It's an
Exploring insight
Into what is and
What is not?

Poetry
What a fascinating
Window unfolding
Any unknown of the
Curious mind

Oh yes,
Poetry what a way
To the illumination of
All that is and more!

Second Thought

Why be
In the world of lies
And deceptions
When we're
The precious gift,
The illumined mind

Why be
Tangled into these
Notions of subjectivity,
And uncertainty
When we got the
Power of clarity,
At will

Why not
Erase obsessions,
False values and ever
Changing
Interpretations and be
Free at- last…

"I"

It's always
That leaps of faith;
Soaring "I" from
Here to the world
Of deeper meaning

Wonder,
What if, "I" locked
Up into such a
Perfect reality

Will "I" be
A radiant Spirit;
Knocking off my old
Earthly habits or what?

Let "I"
Meditate in silence
Let "I" introspect over
My presence in this
Magic milieu

Let "I"
Conquer the long
Overdue big dream;
Illuminating my Sprit...

Love
Never Lies

Oh yes
That sweet face
Always smiling with
Her warm feelings

Every time,
We met either on
The campus or at a
Social

Our inner
Beings had already
Fell in love

Well, our
Respective pride
Refused to give in

So we kept
Dancing; pretending,
"We're just good
Friends…"

What's &
What's not?

If God means,
Goodness, and
If human doesn't

In that case,
Inference is clear,
"God doesn't exists for
Them either"

If Truth means,
"Integrity of the mind"
And if humans doesn't

Well again,
"Truth shall be unknown
To them forever"

If Human
Consistently fails to notice,
"He's been walking along a
Wrong track for a long"

In that case,
He shall never find the way
To his noble goal…"

Moral Adventure

When
We absorb
Our spiritual unity in
This revolving holistic
Reality

At that
Turning point, we shall
Be reborn, "Eternal Essence"
With humility and elegance,
Indeed

That must be
The ultimate experience
That must remain immortal
In our hearts and minds

So let us
All wake-up to the
New reality, to the new
Future and to the new moral
Adventure as directed above...

Forgotten

What should
Be the reciprocity
Between living and
The dead is the

Big question
That keeps revolving
In my inner thoughts

Those who
Passed on, now
In a gold frame and

In time,
The frame collects
Dust and eventually falls
Off the memory wall

As a
Consequence,
Those dead are forgotten
As if they never were...

World Song

Let this
Be the clarion bells
Awakening our Global
Spirit; demanding
To March for Good

Yes,
This is our time
To act, to heal and to
Take a stand for our
Dignity as human beings

Yes, this is
The time to come together
And be concerned for the
Greater good of the whole

We're all in it,
We're fighting against
AIs, Climate, deadly nukes
And much more

Come, let's sing
The Global song, "To save
Life, Planet and future of
Our kids"

Yes the future of
Our kids...damn right the
Future of our kids only..."

New
Dawn

Clarity leads
To understanding
This complex reality
We're in

Clarity of
Thoughts, words and
Inferences

Opens the
Door to the truth
We've been querying
For a long

Time to
Reevaluate beliefs
And determine, their
Validity today

Time to
Grasp the power of
Our collective endeavor
And be the heroes of the
New Dawn...

Invincible

Invincible
Do not tremble over
Trivial things, events
Or any evil

They just
Transcend from here
To the moral depth

It's essentially,
Their way in reaching
Out to the distant stars
For greater inspiration

Invisibles
Never run away
From their commitment
In lifting all souls to the
Brightest North Star...

Let's Fly

Beware,
We're here for a
While in this magnifique
World

Yes,
We're here for a
Brief; leaping from
Unknown to another

All is
Uncertainty and
Struggle yet all is so
Fascinating and the
Glory to be experienced

We're
The lost time travelers
Seeking to know the magic
Of all that is

We're the
Indefatigable born
To fight the illusion, lies
And the seven sin…

Mother's Day

Mother,
Oh yes only the mother
Can inure all the difficulties
Of existence and
Still
Got the courage to live
With love in the world

Mother,
The Goddess who
Never seeks anything,
But to give and sacrifice

Mother,
The ever pious soul
Ready to give her life for
The well being of her kids

Mother,
The pure heart that
Never wants anything in
Return but love

"Happy Mother's Day"
Mom while your spirit is
Still smiling in my heart,
Mind and soul…

Morass

In the
Turmoil of a romance,
Often two souls are
Mixed-up with their
Mistrust and confusion,
"Who they're and how
To lead the way"

What a
Tragic experience
When neither is ready
To "Let Go"

They don't
Seek to listen, but
Simply point fingers
At each other

They want
To talk but they don't
Want to hear what the
Other says

Lovers,
Lacking common sense;
Trying to revive their
Morbid affairs, time after
Time…

That's it

Existence
Moves on every day
And everyway

All is a
Change from here
And beyond

Nothing
Remains and
Nothing must go in
Vain

Existence
What a thin
Life line between
Birth and death

Existence,
What a mighty silent;
Lifting all dreams and
Despair at the
Same time

Existence,
What a "Double-edged
Sword" that cut
Both ways always...

Fulfillment

Lovers
Cannot escape
Consequences of
Their right or wrong

That is the
Fork where their
Love is
Under scrutiny
Every time

That is the
Test of their trust and
Friendship at every
Turning point

Love may be
Sweet and full of
Fantasy yet a soul
Killer too!

Our Quest

From the
Shinning stars,
Let us regain
Self-confidence
For a change

Let us draw
Some wisdom
From their incredible
Illumination and

Relearn,
"How to light-up the
Inner being, today"

Let us
Not just revolve around
The edge

Let us be the
Moral Braves, and hit the
Very core

Come
Let us begin to purify
Our thoughts, words and
Deeds, and touch the shinning
Stars today

Long
Shot

Know how to
Tread well, and stitch
The wounded humanity
In time

Yes, to find
The way to fly high
And be the impossible
Possible alright

Only
The honesty of
Endeavors shall free
Us from the despair

Let us
Bind together all
Dreams, wishes and
Courage to resolve the
Issues of our time

Let us do
Something meaningful
To justify our births
While we're on a noble
Sojourn together ahead...

Inner
Voice

Being
Is the truth of
His inner voice

Being is the
Truth of his own
Moral will to act

Truth
Neither God nor any
Virtue to be embattled

Truth means,
Mind conquering
Lies, deceptions and
False narratives of his/her
Time...

To Be

To be is
To live with an
Integrity of the
Mind

To be is
To be triumphant
Of Good over evil,
Every time

This journey
May be
Rough and tough to
Go through

Still a worthy
Adventure to explore,
"What is unknown to
The solemn soul"

To be is to
Focus on positive
Acts of life, and be the
Real heroes of the time…

Cosmic Fabric

I am
What have I become
Through the passage of
My life and time

I am
Just a walking universe
Moving from one unknown
To another

I must be
All about understanding
The grand unity between
"Self-Truth" and the incredible
Cosmic reality, *sub stratum*

I must be
The intricately woven
Meaning of all that was, all
That is and all that shall be,
Indeed...

Parallax

There is
Neither void nor
Anything full,
But in the mind of
An ever explorer

He simply
Encounters enigmas,
Contradictions and
The double talks of
His time

Nay sayers
Insist not to go
Beyond, but the
Determined will
Insist otherwise

Being caught
Into the swarms of
Antimonies, and
The chaotic milieu
Of mind, and its time
He arises above all...

Our
Beginning

Dear
Heart we meet
Once gain

Seems we've
Been destined
Forever

Dear heart,
I ask you again,,
"Are you sure you
Want this guy?"

I see your
Smiling heart singing,
"I do"

Well, well
That was conversion
Of dream into reality
At that very flash of
A moment thus the journey
Began…

Revival

Shattered
Dreams of yesterday
Still chasing my
Wounded heart today

Yes, they shall
Recur many tomorrows,
But I don't care

For existence
Is all about uncertainty
And not knowing, "Where
Am I heading?"

Time to
Reinvigorate my brave
Soul and time to
Be strong, and

Fight back
To get back the lost
Hope again…

Beware

Dear
Worldly folks,
Let's constraint our
Destructive behavior
And get on the right
Track

Let's accept,
"We've lost our moral
Vigor and succumbed to
The gluttony of materialism
And technoism alright"

What's the point
Of existence,
If we continue to be
The killing machines

Le's wake-up
To the reality of survival
Let's be concern over our
Collective freedom…

Measure of Measure

If a religion
Doesn't got a room
For forgiveness, then
Think twice

If a religion
Doesn't hold progressive
Elements to nourish harmony
And Peace, well then think
Again

If a
Religion doesn't offer
An open mindfulness, and
Treat women as equal;
Politely walk away
At once for your daughters
Sake

If a religion
Keeps peddling false
Narratives and dogmatic
Attitude; use your
Common sense and simply
Walk off the destructive trail…

Dreamers

We're
Dreamers rolling
Along the green terrain
To find our ultimate gem

We're
Brave warriors often
Half-crazy/ half- awakened
Breed

We keep walking
Through the light and dark
At the same time, but not
Knowing where we're heading,
At any time

We're smart,
But we're quite mixed-up
With our conflicting inferences

We've also
Turned into lost souls for
We've lost our identity,

"How to strengthen our
Moral will, and be the winners
At every turning point of
Our existence…"

Declaration

Man declares
To the world,
"I exist, therefore
I am everything"

For him,
He's maker of ethics,
Aesthetics and

Being an ascending
Spirit to the meaning,
"Who is he?"

Like it or not,
He's about
Grief and joy, love,
Truth and many
Mores

Hope
He knows well,
"He exists for a brief."

Trinity

God, Being
And Reality defining
The core essence of
The human thought

God, who
Either exists or not?

Being is he
Either awake or not?

Reality,
Always a binding
Force between chaos and
Order of any time

When
These are corrected
In time; peace remains a
Dominant determinate...

My Query

What is the
Justification of a
Supreme Being

When
Children keep dying
One war after another

What is the
Meaning of life

When humanity
Is constantly under
The Damocles' sword

What is the
Worth of a human
In our time

When
He's lost his social
Responsibility; turning
To be a complete moron…

Epilogue

**There is
No such thing called,
"Illusion," but human
Mind only**

**Reality
Never a mirage, but
Concrete all through**

**Don't say,
"Life got no purpose"
For it
Carries many million
Possibilities**

**Human got
To unfold them
All with the
Moral insight**

**Don't ever
Say,
"Love got no worthy
Meaning"**

**For love offers
A genuine humanity
With dignity, always…**

JAGDISH J. BHATT, PhD

Brings 45 years of academic experience including a post-doctorate research scientist at Stanford University, CA. His total career publications: scientific, educational and literary is nearly100 including over 60 books.